PREPARING CHILDREN for the RITE of RECONCILIATION

First Penance

Lesson One

God Loves Me!

Francine M. O'Connor

This Is the World that God Has Made

I know that God loves me because Jesus told me so. When I see the beautiful things our Creator has made, I remember God's love. I know nothing I do will ever change that love!

How many of God's gifts can you find in this picture?

I woke up this morning and the sun was shining in my window. I heard a little bird singing in the tree outside. It seemed like the bird was saying, "Get up! Get up! God has made a wonderful day!"

And all the beautiful things in my world reminded me of God's love.

I went downstairs to the kitchen where Mother was making breakfast. She placed my breakfast on the table, and, oh, how good it smelled! Then, Mother smiled a special mother smile. "Good morning, sweetheart," she said, and gave me a great big hug and kiss. Daddy came in and lifted me way up high. "Have a wonderful day," he said.

I felt the love of my parents and remembered that God is my loving Father, who watches over me every day.

At school, I read a story all by myself. It was about a little girl and her dog. Then, my teacher helped me with a math problem that I didn't understand. After lunch, we had a spelling bee, and I came in third.

I was so glad that God gave me a mind that can love and learn new things, and a teacher to show me the way.

After school, I went out to play. It was a beautiful day. My best friend came riding by on his brand new bicycle. "Would you like to ride my bike?" he asked. And I said, "Oh, yes, I would." My friend was not afraid that I would break his new bike. He trusted me. So I let him play with my best ball while I took a ride on his bike.

And I remembered that God is the best kind of friend, a very good friend who loves me a lot.

Every time I walk in the park, and see children and flowers and trees and birds, I remember again about God's love for the world and the people on earth.

I learn more about how God loves me when I go to church with my family and hear the words of Jesus and about all the loving things he did for all of God's children — like me.

When I hear how Jesus came to our world just to teach about God's love, I know nothing I do will ever make God stop loving me.

Lesson Two

Mystery Scripture Message

Francine M. O'Connor

Here is a message from the Bible that tells how the people have always felt about God. Unscramble the scrambled words to find out what the message says.

iSgn ljofyu ____________________

osgsn to the ____________________

rodL! moeC to ____________________

wrohspi him ____________________

with tnahkflu ____________________

ehatrs and osgsn ____________________

of parsie. The ____________________

rodL is the ____________________

rgetaest oGd. ____________________

Psalm 95:1,2,3

How I Lov

PRAY SHARE PRAISE

I can love God in so many ways.
Day after day, I am learning new ways to love my wonderful God.

I can love God as a very good *Friend*:
A Friend I can talk to in my prayers, when I am lonely and want company.
Maybe sometimes my Friend is lonely, too.
Then, I will keep my Friend company.

I can tell my Friend all my secrets.
When I am worried about something, I know my Friend will make things right.
Then I can stop worrying.
I can laugh and talk with my Friend when everything is wonderful and I am very happy.
I can share my joy with my Friend.

I can thank my Friend for being there when I need to talk.
I can love God as a very good *Friend*!

I can love God as my *Father* in heaven:
I know my Father watches over me and cares for me every day.
I know my Father never forgets about me.

I can listen to my Father's words and try to follow them.
I can learn the Ten Commandments and always live by them.
I know when I obey, my Father is happy and so am I.

I can be good to friends and neighbors because they are my Father's children, too.
They are my brothers and sisters.
We all belong to one big family.

I can surprise my Father with little presents — saying special prayers of love and doing kind things for others.
I can love God as a caring *Father*!

I can love God as *God*:
I can look around the world and see how great and wonderful God is.
I can go to Mass and listen to the stories of God.

I can believe, when my priest says, "This is my body and this is my blood," that God is truly mysterious and powerful enough to overcome death.

PREPARING CHILDREN for the RITE of RECONCILIATION

First Penance

Lesson Three

Love One Another

Francine M. O'Connor

Jesus loves you very much. He said, "Love one another as I have loved you." Unscramble the words below the pictures to find ways you can love others as Jesus loves you.

TAEHC AOBTU OGD

FDEE HET ORPO

VSITI TEH CSKI

RPYA

FROGVIE OERTSH

LOVE AS JE

You can learn how to love by reading

When Jesus was a little boy, he obeyed Mary and Joseph. When he grew up, he did what his Father sent him to do. He suffered and died for us. He told his Father, "I will do it your way."

You can love as Jesus loves.

You can listen to your parents and do the things they ask of you. You can remember how they love you and you can love them back. When what your parents ask seems hard to do, remember what Jesus told his Father, and do it their way.

When people had a physical disability, or were sick, Jesus made them well again.

You can love as Jesus loves.

You can visit people who are sick, you can make cards, or write letters to cheer them up.

When the people were hungry, Jesus multiplied the loaves and fish so everyone had enough to eat.

You can love as Jesus loves.

You can give food or clothes to people who help the poor. You can share your toys with friends.

WORDS

HIDDEN IN THIS S
THAT TELL YOU HO
LOVE. SEE IF YO

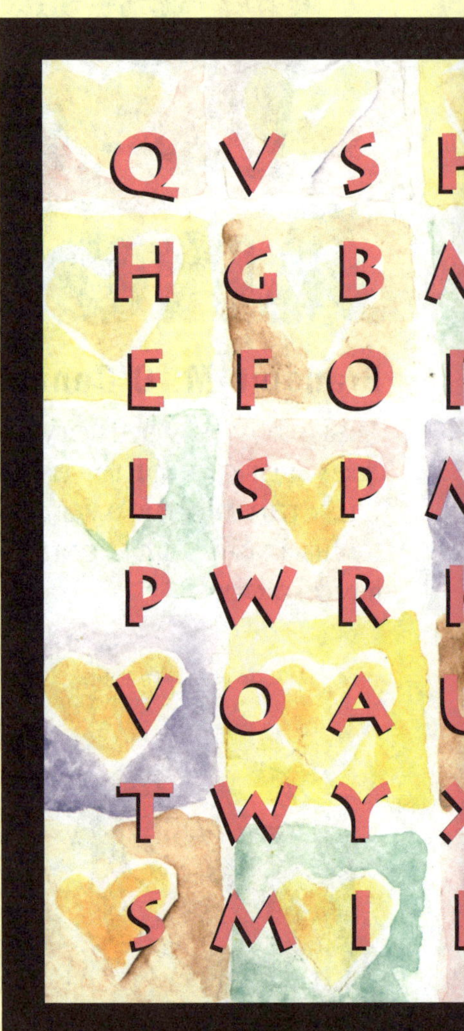

WO

SHARE · HELP · FOR

Lesson Four

1. You shall honor no other god but me.
(Always put God first in everything you do.)

2. You shall not misuse the name of the Lord your God.
(God's name is a prayer. Always say it with love.)

3. Remember to keep holy the Sabbath day.
(Celebrate with Jesus every week in holy Mass.)

4. Honor your father and your mother.
(Obey and help your parents.)

5. You shall not kill.
(Always be kind to others.)

6. You shall not commit adultery.
(Be loyal to your family and friends.)

7. You shall not steal.
(Take care of things that belong to others.)

8. You shall not bear false witness against your neighbor.
(Tell only good and truthful things about others.)

9. You shall not covet your neighbor's wife.
(Don't be jealous of other friendships.)

10. You shall not covet your neighbor's goods.
(Don't be jealous of what others have.)

God wants us to stay close. But we need to know how to do this. So God gave us directions to follow. These directions are called the Ten Commandments or God's Rules.

Jesus added two more rules.

You shall love the Lord your God with all your heart, with all your soul, and with all your mind.

You shall love your neighbor as yourself.

If we follow these two Great Rules, we will have no problem following the Ten Commandments.

It's All A

Jenny was very, very worried. She loved God with all her heart. But sometimes things happened that Jenny just couldn't help. Once she broke her brother's toy when she was playing with it. And when she painted a picture for Dad, she spilled paint on the living room rug. Jenny thought God wouldn't love her. These were such terrible sins.

Oh, but Jenny was very wrong! It was an accident when she broke the toy. It was a mistake to paint in the living room. *Accidents and mistakes are not sins.* You cannot commit a sin by accident. You cannot commit a sin by mistake. You always have a choice: *To love or not to love!* You sin when you choose not to love. God's rules teach you how to love.

Think about God every day.
Remember to say your prayers.
Obey the first commandment.

God's name is a holy name.
Use God's name in thanks for God's love.
Obey the second commandment.

Be with Jesus at holy Mass.
Make Sunday a special God-day.
Obey the third commandment.

Be a kind and helpful child at home.
Love your parents with all your heart.
Obey the fourth commandment.

Never hurt anyone on purpose.
Treat your friends and neighbors kindly.
Obey the fifth commandment.

Remember that your family is holy.
Be loving and good to each other.
Obey the sixth commandment.

Take care of things that belong to others.
Always return toys you have borrowed.
Obey the seventh commandment.

Don't tell lies about others.
Always say good and truthful things.
Obey the eighth commandment.

Don't be jealous of other friendships.
Every person is special in different ways.
Obey the ninth commandment.

Don't be jealous of what others have.
Be happy with what God has given you.
Obey the tenth commandment.

You are God's very special child.
Nothing can change God's love for you —
not accidents, not mistakes, not even sins!
Always remember God's rules of love!

PREPARING CHILDREN for the RITE of RECONCILIATION

First Penance

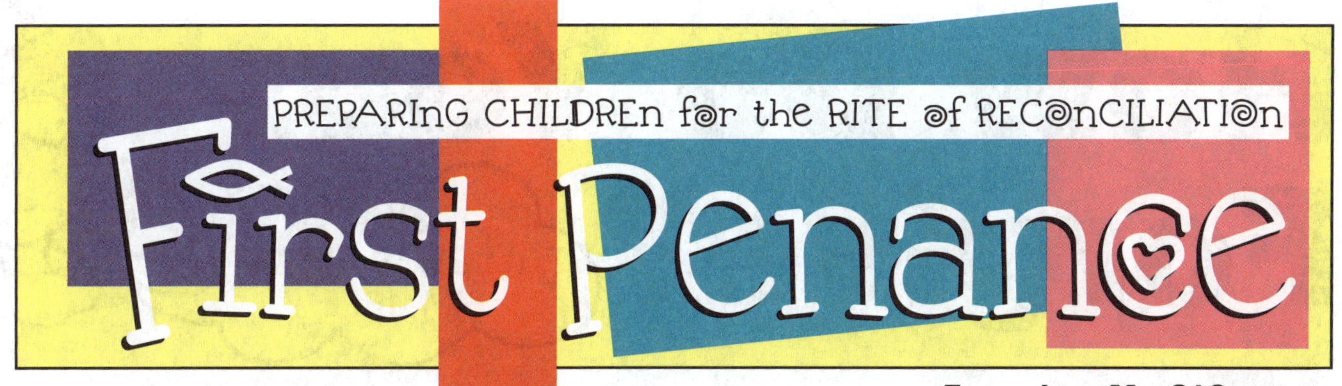

Francine M. O'Connor

Lesson Five

Jesus *Forgives* a Sinner

A SHORT MAN NAMED ZACCHAEUS climbed up in a tree, trying to see Jesus over the crowd. He was not always a good man. He became rich by cheating people. Jesus said, "Come down. I am going to your house today." People were surprised. Jesus forgave Zacchaeus for his sins. Zacchaeus wanted to be better for Jesus. He gave back all the money he had stolen, which pleased the people. This story has a happy ending for everyone — Jesus forgave Zacchaeus and Zacchaeus was ready to begin anew.

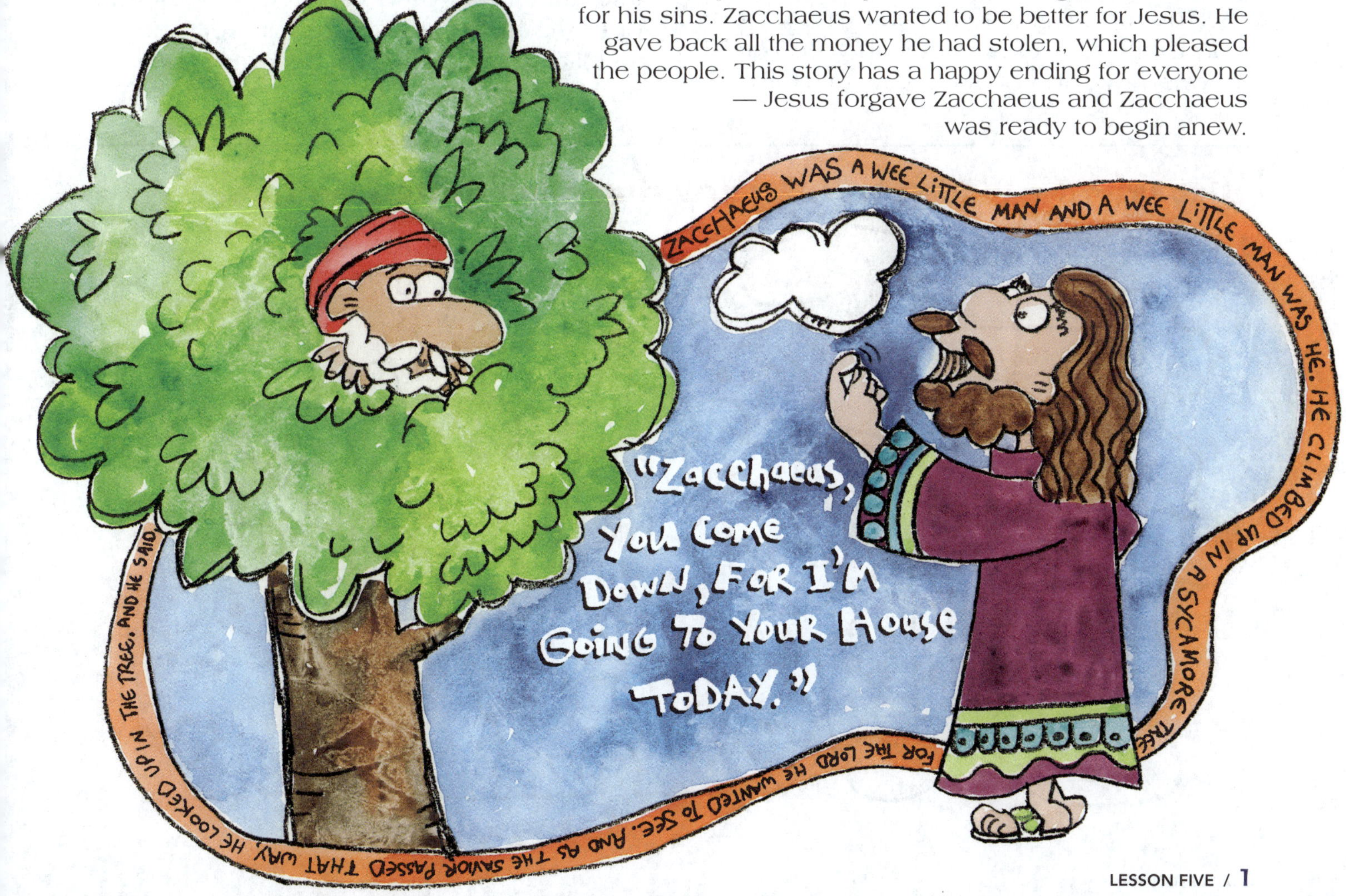

How Do You Forgive?

I JUST FOLLOWED JESUS' EXAMPLE.

The story of Zacchaeus is a story with a happy ending. Jesus knew a very important secret: Stories about forgiving always have happy endings and always lead to new beginnings.

You and your best friend have had a fight. Your friend won't speak to you. Think about how terrible you feel. Now think about how good you feel when you call to say, "I'm sorry," and your friend says, "I'm sorry, too." You become best friends again. Your story has a happy ending and a new beginning.

You have done something wrong. Your mother is very upset with you. Think about how sad you feel. Now think about how good you feel when your mother comes to you with a happy smile or a big hug. Even without words, you know you have been forgiven. You want to do something nice for her. Your story has a happy ending and a new beginning.

There are many ways to forgive. Every way leads to a happy ending and a new beginning. When you forgive someone or when someone forgives you, you both get a chance to start over. Friendships become just like new, families become close again, and sadness turns into gladness. When you forgive someone or someone forgives you, you become just like Zacchaeus. You become a better and happier you.

Discover the hidden word by coloring each dotted section.

PREPARING CHILDREN for the RITE of RECONCILIATION

First Penance

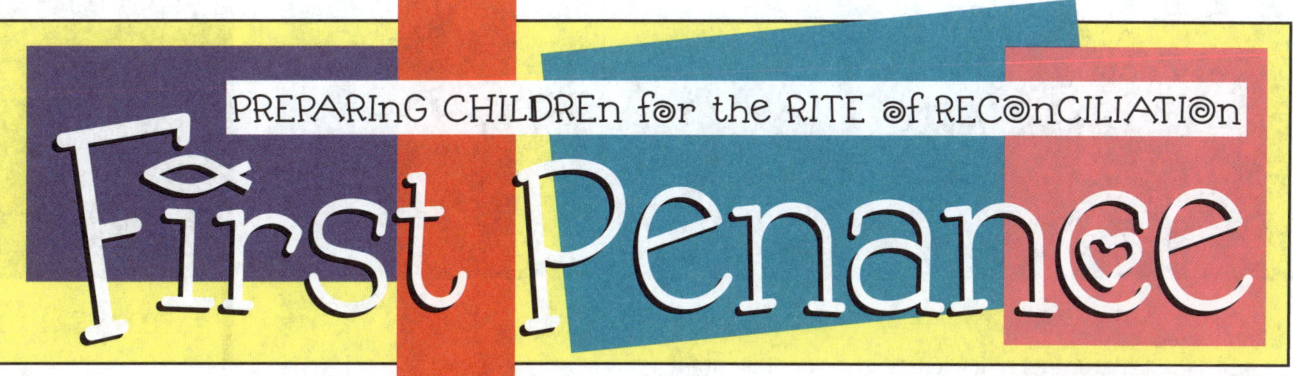

Francine M. O'Connor

Lesson Six

Coming Home Again

Have you ever been away from home overnight?
Can you remember how it felt to come home again?
Jesus has a "Welcome Home" surprise for you
this week in his story of the
boy who ran away.

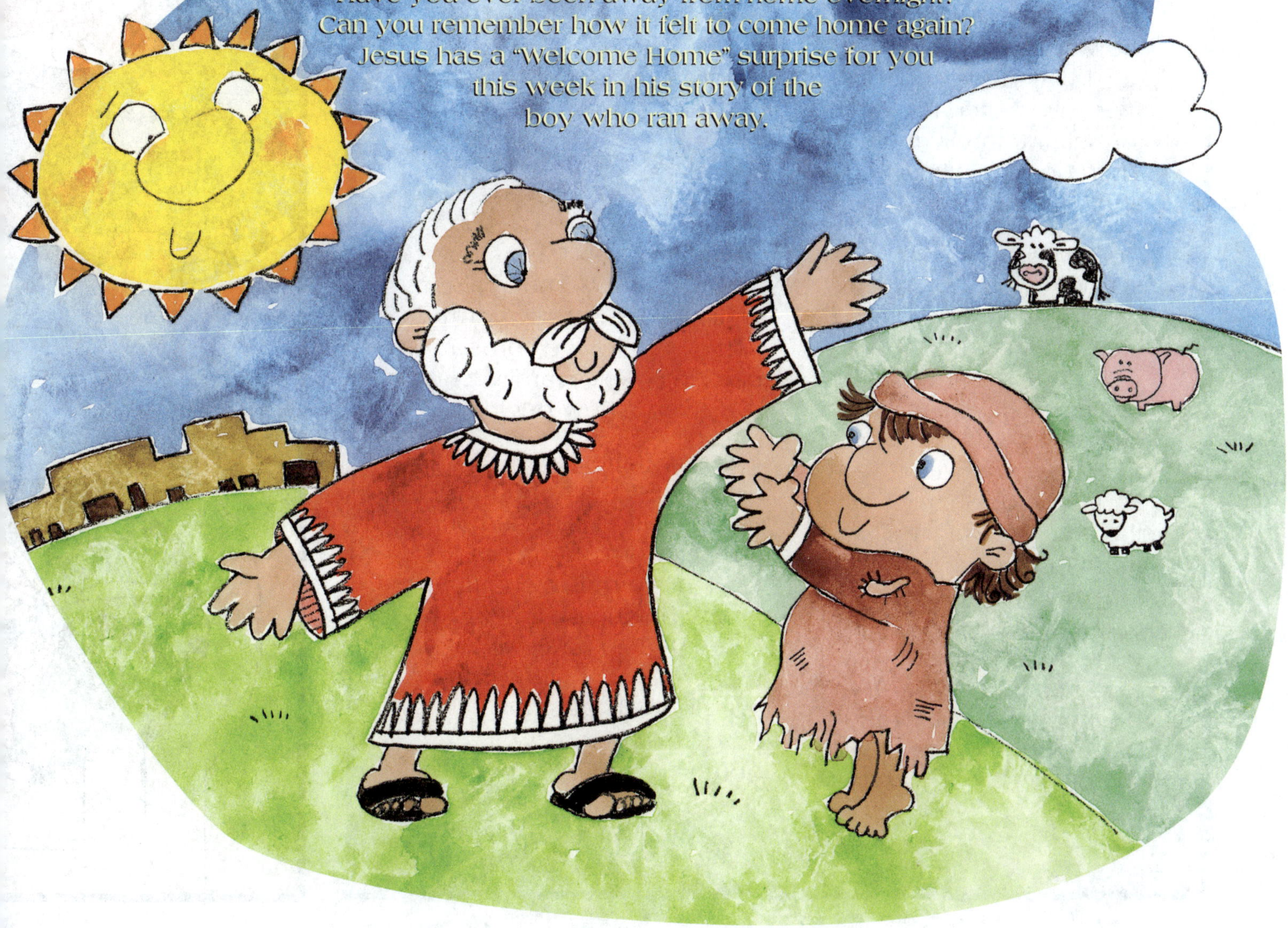

A Jesus Love Story

Have you ever wondered, "Does God still love me when I do something wrong?" Jesus told a story about God's love. It is a story of love that never changes.

A man had two sons. The younger son was not happy working on his father's farm. "I want to see the world," he thought. "I don't want to spend my life here." He asked his father for half the family money. Then he took all his things and left home.

He had a great time spending his money. He had many friends to help him. But when his money was gone, his friends disappeared. He was all alone. He wandered from town to town. He begged for his food. He slept out in the cold and rain. He thought about his father's farm, about the warm fire and his father's love. He decided to go home. "I will tell my father I am sorry," he thought. "I will work hard for him if he will take me back."

The father saw the boy coming down the road. He ran out and hugged him and kissed him. "Father, I have sinned against God and you," said the son. "I do not deserve to be your son."

But the father was so happy to see him, he said to his servants, "Let us celebrate, for my son has come back to me."

This story is really about God. God is the loving Father. When you have sinned, God doesn't stop loving you. God waits for you to come home again; waits for you to say you're sorry. You are welcomed back into God's family. You are given a new beginning.

You are getting ready to receive the sacrament of reconciliation. This is your time to "come home" to God. It is a making-up time, a new beginning time. God loves you so much, that no matter how far away you go, God will always be ready to welcome you home.

PREPARING CHILDREN for the RITE of RECONCILIATION

First Penance

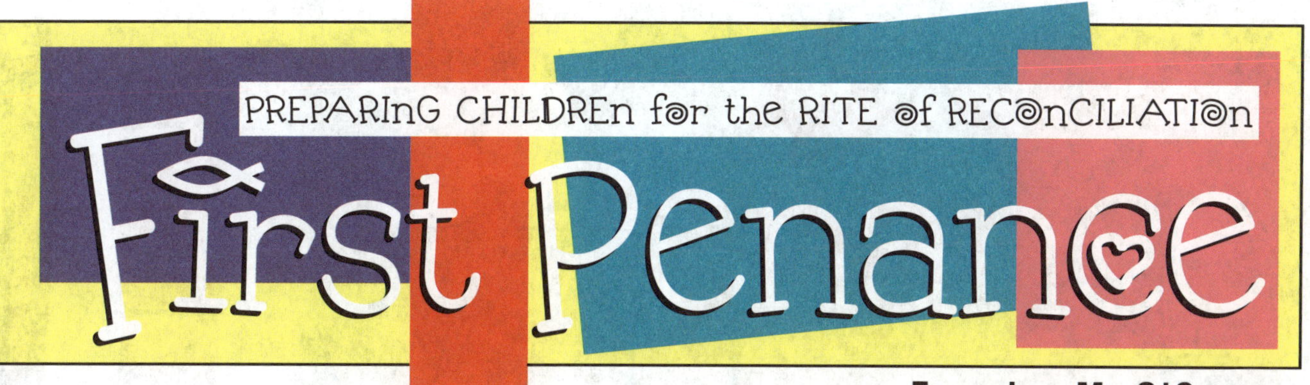

Francine M. O'Connor

Lesson Seven

FAMILIES WORK TOGETHER

When a family works together, things get done — and everyone feels happy and proud.

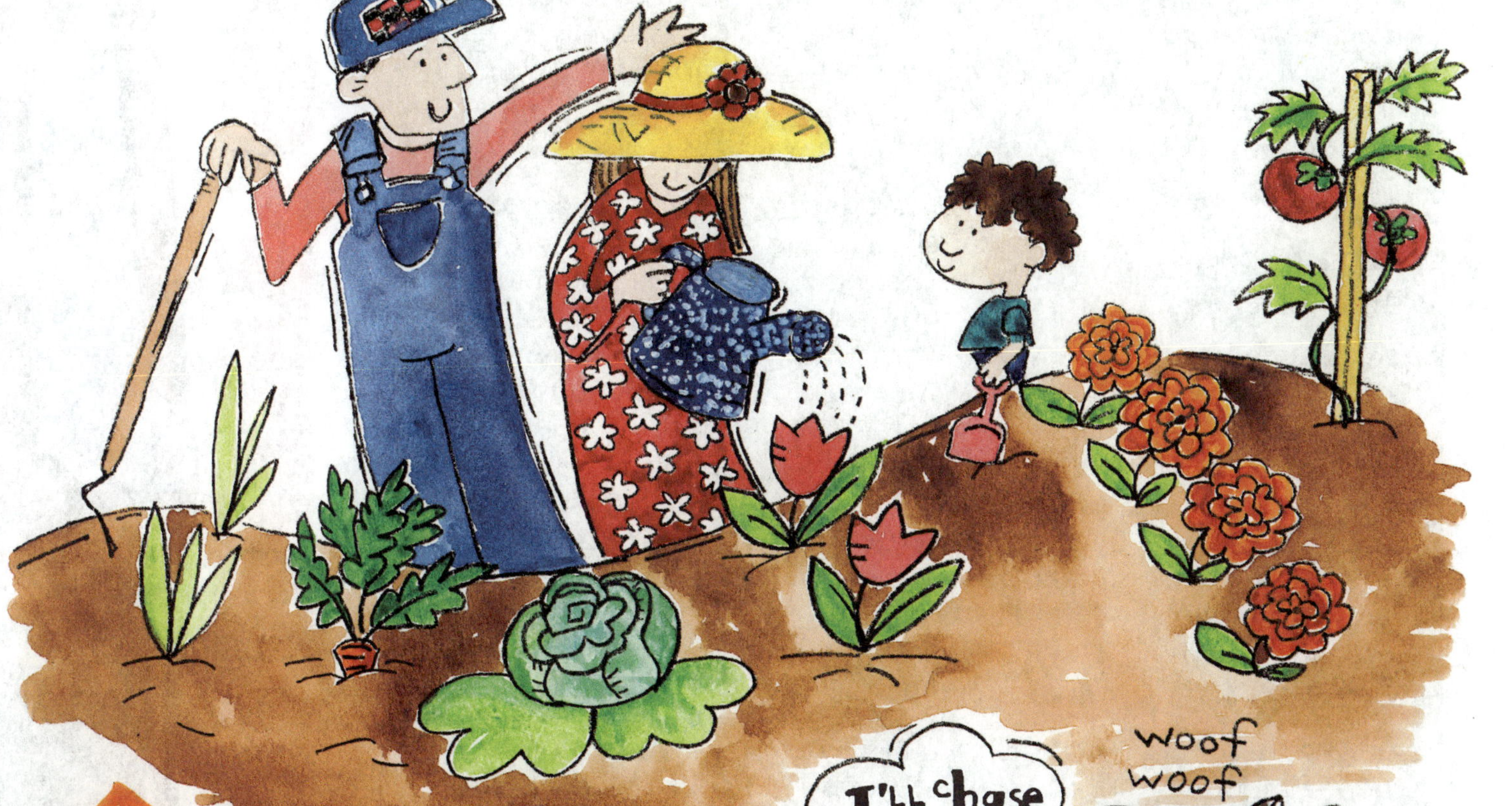

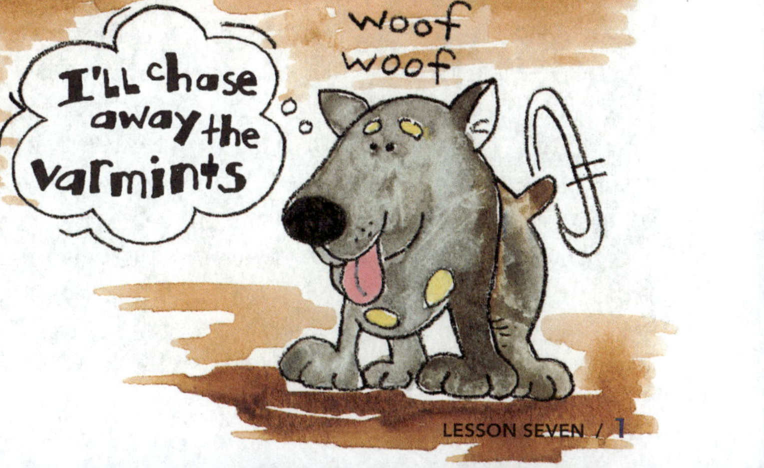

woof woof
I'll chase away the varmints

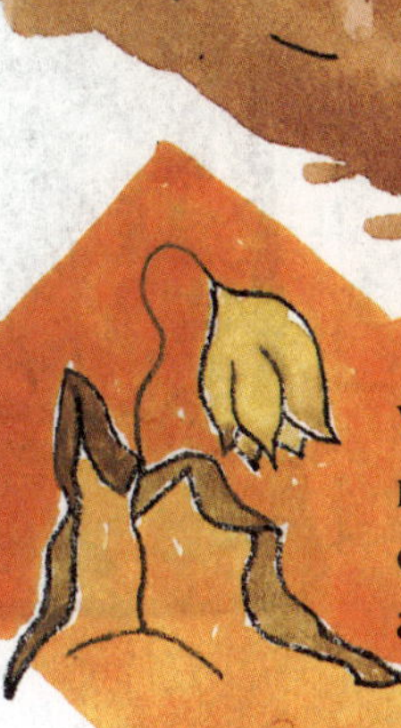

When someone in the family is not loving and kind to the others, nothing gets done — and everyone feels unhappy.

You Are Family

THE BODY OF CHRIST

You belong to a family. In your family, you learn to love, to care, and to forgive. You do things together. You share the work of making a nice home. You celebrate special days together.

Everyone in your family has a very important place. Everyone is needed to make the family whole. When each person in the family is helpful and loving and kind, the whole family is happy.

But what happens when someone is not loving or forgiving? The whole family is hurt. Do you know the magic words that can make you happy again? The magic words are: "I'm sorry" and "I forgive you!" All loving families know these magic words.

You also belong to God's family. You became a member of God's family the day you were baptized. You do many important things with others in God's family. You worship together at Mass. You listen to God's Word. You celebrate important days together.

In God's family, you also learn to love, to care, and to forgive. Jesus said, "Whenever you did it for any of my people...you did it for me" (Mt 25:40). When you help others, it is like helping Jesus. And God's family is happy and proud.

Jesus also said, "Whenever you failed to help any of my people...you failed to do it for me" (Mt 25:45). Therefore, when you refuse to help others, it is the same as refusing to help Jesus. And God's family feels sad.

But again, we can use the magic words. In the sacrament of reconciliation, we say, "I'm sorry," and Jesus says, "I forgive you." And God's family is happy again.

PREPARING CHILDREN for the RITE of RECONCILIATION

First Penance

Francine M. O'Connor

Lesson Eight

A Brand New Beginning

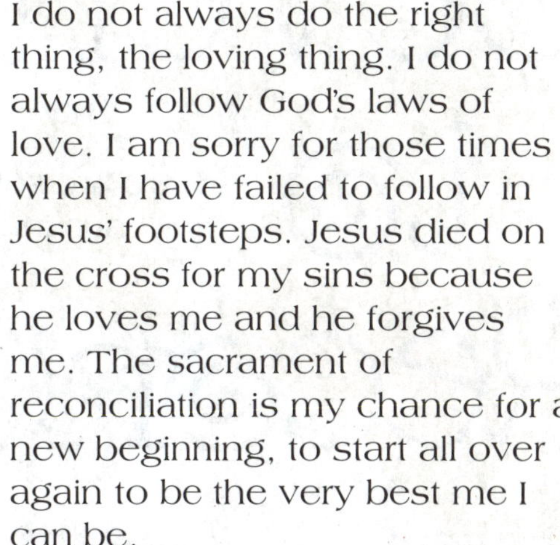

I do not always do the right thing, the loving thing. I do not always follow God's laws of love. I am sorry for those times when I have failed to follow in Jesus' footsteps. Jesus died on the cross for my sins because he loves me and he forgives me. The sacrament of reconciliation is my chance for a new beginning, to start all over again to be the very best me I can be.

Below is a prayer I will say each night to tell God I am sorry.

An Act of Contrition

O my God, I love you above all things.

I am truly sorry for all my sins,

and I thank you for forgiving me.

Help me to stay close to you

and to remember always

your wonderful laws of love. Amen

Celebrate R

How You Receive the Sacrament of Reconciliation

You can choose one of two ways to go to confession. You can kneel before a screen that separates you from the priest, or you can sit in a chair and talk to the priest face-to-face. It is entirely up to you. The steps you follow to celebrate this sacrament are the same whether you choose to talk to the priest face-to-face or through the screen.

Seven Steps to Reconciliation

Here are seven easy steps to tell your sins to Jesus in the sacrament of reconciliation:

1. Father will greet you when you enter the confessional or reconciliation room. Together, you will make the *Sign of the Cross*.

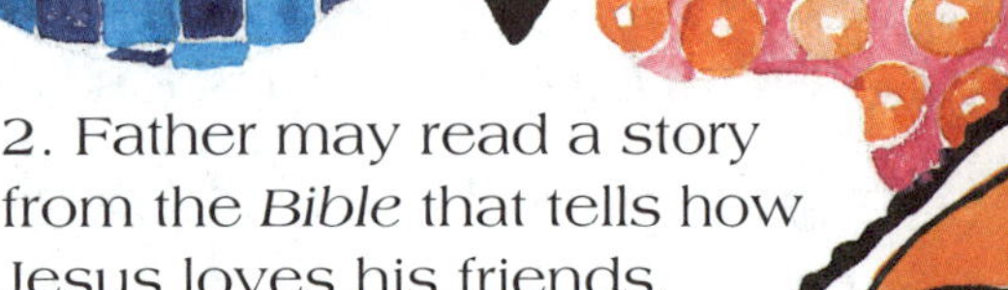

2. Father may read a story from the *Bible* that tells how Jesus loves his friends.

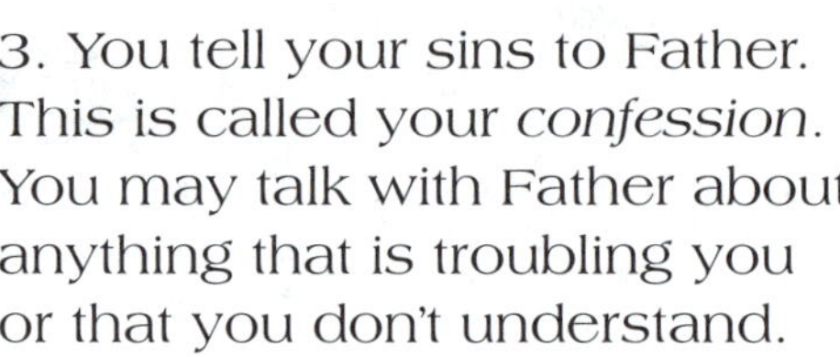

3. You tell your sins to Father. This is called your *confession*. You may talk with Father about anything that is troubling you or that you don't understand.

orgiveness

A happy day is coming soon. It is your day to receive the sacrament of reconciliation.

This is the day that you will say to Jesus those wonderful words: "I am sorry!"

Jesus will speak to you through the priest and say those wonderful words: "I forgive you and love you!"

This is your day to begin again, your day to make the promise, "I will try not to sin anymore." What a happy day for you! What a happy day for God! What a happy day for God's family!

4. Father will ask you to do something special to show Jesus you are sorry for your sins. This is called your *penance*.

5. You say a prayer telling Jesus you are sorry for your sins. This prayer is called an *Act of Contrition*.

6. Father will pray for you and say the words of forgiveness. This is called *absolution*.

7. You and Father *thank* Jesus together for his wonderful gift of forgiveness.

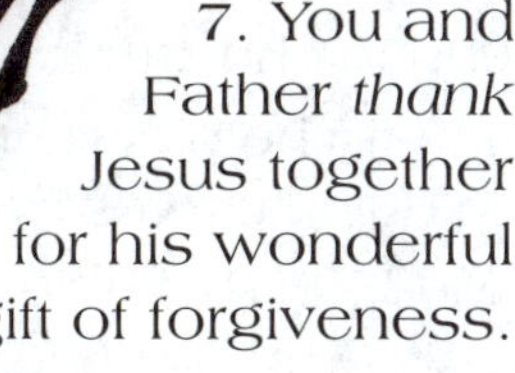

To the Teacher

An Examination of Conscience

Based on the Ten Commandments and Jesus' two great commandments.

Create a quiet atmosphere in the classroom for the examination of conscience. Light a candle as a sign of God's presence. You might have instrumental music playing softly in the background.

Explain to the children that this will help them prepare to receive the sacrament of reconciliation. Begin with a prayer or a reading from Scripture. After the children seem settled, lead the class through the examination, pausing for a short while after each question to allow time for reflection.

- Do I love God as a child of God?
- Do I remember to pray every day?
- Do I thank God for all God has done for me?
- Do I always say God's name with love?
- Do I show my love for God by loving others?
- Do I keep Sunday holy by going to Mass?
- Do I listen carefully to God's Word at Mass?
- Do I remind myself that I am in God's house and behave as I should?
- Do I always talk nicely to my parents?
- Do I do what my parents ask me to do?
- Do I help with chores around the house?
- Do I try to be pleasant while doing chores and obeying my parents?
- Do I show my love for others by obeying my parents?
- Do I show my love for others by obeying rules at school and at public places?
- Do I treat others with love and kindness?
- Do I ever hurt others by calling them names?
- Do I fight with others?
- Do I always tell the truth?
- Do I ever make promises that I do not keep?
- Do I ever cheat on tests or schoolwork?
- Do I take things that do not belong to me?
- Do I refuse to share my things with others?
- Do I treat the property of others with respect and care?

To the Parents

The children have learned to make a thorough examination of conscience in preparation for the sacrament of reconciliation. This is a big step in your child's life. This week, have the whole family work together to compose a prayer service especially geared to your family and to your celebration of the wonderful forgiveness of God.

Open with a song of joy and love for Jesus. Have the leader read one of the forgiveness stories from the Bible. The Prodigal Son, the story of Zacchaeus, and the Lost Sheep are all good examples (Lk 15:11-24; Lk 19:1-10; Lk 15:4-7).

Compose a litany of thanksgiving for what God has forgiven you in the past. For example, "For the times we have been selfish," (respond) "Lord Jesus, thank you for your forgiving love." Close your prayer service by saying an Act of Contrition together.

From the *Catechism of the Catholic Church*

#1423-24 on the meanings of the sacrament of penance

#1451-53 on contrition

#1454 on the examination of conscience

#1468-69 on the effects of the sacrament of penance

Editor: Lauren K. Borstell.
Art and design: Christine Kraus.
Published with ecclesiastical approval.
Phone: 800-325-9521. Web: Liguori.org.

Another name for God's family is the Body of Christ. God's family is like a body, with Jesus as the head. Just as the parts of your body can do special helpful things, each member of God's family can also do special, helpful things. Write ways that you obey God's commandment with these parts of your body.

Hands

With my hands I can ____

____.

Legs

With my legs I can ____

____.

Mouth

With my mouth I can ____

____.

Ears

With my ears I can ____

____.

Eyes

With my eyes I can ____

____.

To the Teacher

Although the full meaning of the Body of Christ is beyond the children's comprehension at this age, the idea can help them understand that their sins hurt everyone. Reconciliation brings them into union not only with God but with the whole Church. The following activity should help bring this message home to the children.

The Serve or Sin Project

1. Begin by having the children tell of times when one part of their bodies has been hurt. Help them realize how that one injured part brought pain to the whole body. Ask them to tell the class how good it felt when the injury was well again.
2. Draw and cut out a large poster-board replica of a child's body. Do not draw a face on the head.
3. Ask the children to suggest ways in which the different parts of the body can serve God and others. Write these down on their respective parts on one side of the body, using a marker or crayon.
4. Ask the children to suggest ways in which the different parts of the body can hurt God and others through sin. Turn the body over and write these down on their respective parts.
5. Show the children the "sin" side of the body. Add a sad face and write, "Sin" in large letters on the body. Ask them if they know how to make all those sins go away. Tell them that when they go to confession and receive the sacrament of reconciliation, all the sins disappear.
6. Turn the body over to the other side, add a smiling face, and write, "Serve" in large letters on the body.

Editor: Lauren K. Borstell.
Art and design: Christine Kraus.
Published with ecclesiastical approval.

Printed in U.S.A. Phone: 800-325-9521. Web: Liguori.org.

To the Parents

The best classroom for learning this week's lesson is the home. As the children approach the actual reception of the sacrament of reconciliation, they need to recognize how their sins affect others. Your child will be better able to absorb both the pain of being at odds with the family and the joy of becoming reconciled.

You can emphasize this by using a "reconciliation" box this week. Decorate a small box (a shoe box or empty cereal carton) with the words, "We are reconciled!" Have each member of the family write on small pieces of paper apologies for things he or she has done to interfere with family unity ("I'm sorry I didn't help with the dishes last night;" or "I'm sorry I fought with Johnny on Monday;" or "I'm sorry I was too busy to listen to Jenny's problems"). These can be placed in the box during the week.

At the end of the week, after a prayer for family love and forgiveness, remove the papers and read them aloud. As each one is read, have the injured party say, "I forgive you." Then close the week with a family celebration of togetherness, preferably something you have planned together — such as a special meal, a cake and hot chocolate party, a family game, or a songfest.

From the Catechism of the Catholic Church

- #1333 on the signs of the bread and wine
- #1396 on the Eucharist and the Mystical Body
- #1655-58 on the family of God
- #2206 on family as a privileged community
- #2215 on respect of children for parents

come Home!

back to God through this maze? Be careful not to take the wrong road.

To the Teacher

This week the class can begin work on a poster to celebrate their homecoming on the day they receive the sacrament of penance. If possible, use their "Welcome Home" poster as part of their first penance celebration.

You will need:

- Large sheet of poster board
- Colored construction paper
- Glue
- Scissors
- Markers
- Old magazines

1. Using different colors of construction paper, have the children cut out the letters for the words, "Welcome Home."
2. Glue these letters across the top of your poster.
3. Have the children look through magazines to find pictures of families celebrating together, people coming home from journeys, children playing together, and so forth. Any picture that illustrates people showing love to each other will do.
4. Let the children add their pictures to the poster.
5. With the markers, have each child sign his or her name to the poster.
6. Hang the poster in a central place in the classroom.

Editor: Lauren K. Borstell.
Art and design: Christine Kraus.
Published with ecclesiastical approval.

Printed in U.S.A. Phone: 800-325-9521. Web: Liguori.org.

To the Parents

We can all probably recall a certain reluctance to go to confession in our childhood. Our repentance was stressed, but the love that surrounds the sacrament was somehow lost. It is important for your child to identify the loving father figure in the Prodigal Son story with the forgiving God who is about to touch his or her life with forgiveness and reconciliation.

It is at this point in the preparation of this sacrament that your child learns to anticipate, rather than fear, this encounter with Christ's love. To help your child understand God's love and the joy of reconciliation, talk about how sad you feel when he or she is away from home for any length of time and how good it is when you are together again. If possible, visit or call a relative or friend you haven't seen in a long time. Help your child identify the joy of the family at this reconciliation with the joy of reconciliation with God.

From the *Catechism of the Catholic Church*

- #545 on the kingdom of God
- #1423-24 on the sacrament of penance
- #1439 on conversion and repentance
- #1700 on the dignity of the human person

Jesus Wants You To Forgive

Do you know the Lord's Prayer? In this special prayer that Jesus gave us, he tells us about forgiveness. Do you know the words in the prayer that talk about forgiveness? Write them on the lines below.

When you pray these words, you are asking God to forgive you in the same way that you forgive others. Write some of the ways that you forgive others on the lines below.

To the Teacher

Zacchaeus made a new beginning because Jesus forgave him for his sins. Forgiveness always leads to a new beginning. This week, as a class, celebrate the miracle of forgiveness with a prayer service. In preparation, have each child write a note of forgiveness to someone who has hurt him or her in the past.

A Celebration of Forgiveness

If possible, gather the class in a circle. In the center of the circle, or in some other place of honor, set a candle and a Bible, opened to Luke 19. Begin your prayer service by lighting the candle. Have everyone hold hands and sing a song about forgiveness and Christian love.

Opening Litany

Leader: Father, we are sometimes selfish, and we fail to love and forgive as we should.

All: Lead us to a new beginning, Lord.

Leader: Father, we forgive each other as you have forgiven us.

All: Lead us to a new beginning, Lord.

Leader: Father, we rid ourselves of anger, grudges, and judgments.

All: Lead us to a new beginning, Lord.

Reading

The story of Zacchaeus, Luke 19:1-10

The Lord's Prayer (may be said or sung)

Our Father who art in heaven, hallowed be thy name. Thy kingdom come. Thy will be done on earth, as it is in heaven. Give us this day our daily bread, and forgive us our trespasses as we forgive those who trespass against us, and lead us not into temptation, but deliver us from evil. Amen

Intercessions

Encourage, but don't force, the children to read their forgiveness letters. After each letter is read, the rest of the class should make the following response:

Forgive us our trespasses as we forgive those who trespass against us.

To close your celebration, hold hands and repeat the song of forgiveness you began with, or use another song of Christian love. Then give each other a sign of peace — a handshake or a hug, whichever the children are most comfortable with.

To the Parents

This week, the children are concentrating on forgiveness. Sometimes it is more difficult to forgive each other within the family than it is with friends. Your child will learn more about forgiveness by your example than through any classroom teaching, but don't assume that implied forgiveness is understood. Say it. And when you have done something to hurt your child, you, too, should ask for forgiveness.

Help your child see that giving or receiving forgiveness is a joyful thing. To celebrate family reconciliation, adapt the above prayer service to fit into your family situation. Follow the service with a meal or a cake decorated especially for the occasion.

From the Catechism of the Catholic Church

- #1441, #2839-41 on forgiveness of sins
- #2712 on contemplative prayer
- #2844-45 on forgiveness of others

Editor: Lauren K. Borstell
Art and design: Christine Kraus

…out Love

Accidents, Mistakes, and Sins

Do you know the difference between an accident, a mistake, and a sin? Look at these pictures. Put a big A by the accident, a big M by the mistake, and a big S by the sin.

To the Teacher

Mt 22:34-40; Ex 20:1-17; Dt 5:6-21; Mk 12:28-34; Lk 10:25-28

It is important that children know not only what actions are sins but also what actions are not sins (accidents, mistakes, bad manners, and so forth). Talk to them about things you have done that were accidents or mistakes. Explain that these things made you feel sorry and tell them what you did to make up for them. Once you have established the difference between accidents and sins, have the children answer the questions after each story.

Janie Finds a Dollar

Janie and Mary are very good friends. One day at school, Janie was very sad. She wanted to buy her mother a birthday present, but she didn't have any money. Mary was sad too. Her mother had given her a dollar for lunch money, but she had lost it. When Janie put on her coat to leave that afternoon, she saw Mary's dollar on the floor. Mary didn't see the dollar. "A dollar would buy a nice present for her mother," Janie thought. Mary would never know that Janie found the money.

What do you think Janie should do? What would you do? What would be the love choice? Would it be a sin if Janie kept the money?

Timmy Takes a Ride

Johnny had a new bike. He asked Timmy if he wanted to take a ride. Timmy was very excited about riding Johnny's new bike. He hopped on and rode around the block twice. Each time he passed Johnny, they waved at each other. The third time around the block, a dog came running at Timmy, snapping at his heels. Timmy got so scared he tipped over the bike. The beautiful blue paint got all scratched. Timmy felt like crying. Maybe if he didn't say anything, Johnny would never notice.

Did Timmy commit a sin when he damaged Johnny's bike? Should Timmy tell Johnny about the accident? Can you think of something Timmy can do to make up for scratching Johnny's bike?

Lucy Fails a Test

Lucy has a hard time with arithmetic. Often her answers are wrong. One afternoon, the teacher asked Lucy to come up to the front of the classroom and write an example on the blackboard. Lucy was very scared, but she tried. And guess what? The answer was wrong, just like she feared. She was afraid the teacher would be angry. She thought the class would laugh or that God would be disappointed in her. Lucy was embarrassed.

Did Lucy commit a sin when she got the problem wrong? How would you feel if you were Lucy? How do you think God feels about Lucy's mistake?

To the Parents

The children are learning the difference between mistakes, accidents, and sins. You can underline this message at home every time your child makes a mistake, has an accident, or commits a sin. The important thing is for your child to begin to form a right conscience.

There is a delicate balance between awareness of wrongdoing and a sense of guilt for every little thing that goes wrong. Once your child understands that he or she cannot commit a sin by accident or mistake — that sin requires a decision — this balance will be struck. But it isn't always easy for children to understand this.

To identify the difference, each evening discuss the events of the day with your child. Make notes of both the positive and negative experiences of the day.

Discuss each action with your child. Help make it clear that in order to sin one must first know the difference between right and wrong — and then choose to do the wrong thing. Emphasize the difference between sin and mistakes or accidents. Reinforce the positive actions taken.

From the Catechism of the Catholic Church

- #1749-54 on judgments as good or bad
- #1783-85 on the formation of conscience
- #1846-48 on mercy and sin
- #1849-51 on the definition of sin
- #2052-55 on the Ten Commandments and the Great Commandment

Editor: Lauren K. Borstell.
Art and design: Christine Kraus.
Published with ecclesiastical approval.

Phone: 800-325-9521. Web: Liguori.org.

SUS·LOVES

t the ways that Jesus showed his love.

F LOVE

RE ARE SIX WORDS SUS WANTS YOU TO N FIND ALL SIX.

LIST

· LOVE · SMILE · PRAY

When people did something wrong, Jesus forgave them. He told them, "Sin no more."

You can love as Jesus loves.

When someone hurts your feelings, you can say, "I forgive you." You can always be kind to others and treat them as friends.

Jesus taught in the Temple. He told the people about God's love. He made them happy by reminding them that God is their loving Father.

You can love as Jesus loves.

When your friends are unhappy, you can tell them you love them. You can plan a special surprise to make them happy again.

Jesus went off all by himself to pray to his Father. When he sat down to dinner, he would thank his Father for the food. And when he wanted to help others, he would say a little prayer.

You can love as Jesus loves.

You can remember to say your prayers every day and at every meal. You can pray for others who are sad or who need special help from God.

To the Teacher

Be a Good Samaritan

Luke 10:25-37

Jesus told the story of the Good Samaritan to teach us how we should love one another. Each of us is called upon to be a "Good Samaritan" in his or her own life. The entire week can be "Good Samaritan Week." The whole class can work on ways to follow Jesus' command that we love one another. Follow the steps below to initiate the program, then let the children take over.

You will need:

- An 8-1/2" X 11" sheet of paper for each child
- Crayons or markers
- Gold Stars

1. Give each child a sheet of paper. Have them make calendars with "Good Samaritan Week" written across the top.

2. Have the children fold their papers up from the bottom to the edge of the "Good Samaritan" heading. Now fold the paper in half two times, lengthwise. Unfold. The paper will be divided into eight squares. On the top of each of the first seven squares, have the children write the days of the week.

3. Read the story of the Good Samaritan to the class.

4. Have a discussion period during which the children discuss ways in which they have been Good Samaritans in the past.

5. Select seven love-acts from their discussions (helping, sharing, forgiving, and so forth). Have them write one of these acts in the block for each day this week.

6. Tell the children that this week they are to concentrate on a daily love-act. Have them hang their copies of the calendar at home where they will see them every day. Be sure they know they will have to return the calendars at the end of the week.

7. Each time they carry out a love-act, tell them to write it down in the block for that day — or they can put a star or smiling face in the block.

8. At the end of the week, have the children turn in their calendars. If they have succeeded in carrying out their love-acts, write "Good Samaritan Award" in the empty block and decorate it with a gold star.

To the Parents

This is "Good Samaritan Week." The children will bring home "Good Samaritan" calendars. It will be up to you to see that the work, which started in the classroom, is carried out during the week.

Study your child's calendar to see what he or she will be trying to do each day. Give your child opportunities to perform individual love-acts of your own. Choose a night to have a "Good Samaritan" dinner. Let your child plan and help with the meal. Invite a neighbor or relative, perhaps someone who lives alone, to your dinner.

Or you can have a "Good Samaritan" evening during which the whole family writes letters or makes cards for someone who is ill or lonely.

Please see to it that your child returns his or her calendar to class at the end of the week.

From the Catechism of the Catholic Church

- #520 on imitation of Jesus
- #615 on Jesus' obedience
- #1503-5 on Jesus as physician
- #1509 on our duty to heal
- #2607-15 Jesus teaches how to pray

Editor: Lauren K. Borstell.
Art and design: Christine Kraus.
Published with ecclesiastical approval.

Phone: 800-325-9521. Web: Liguori.org.

I can praise God in my prayers.
I can say every single day how wonder-filled God is.
I can give thanks for the world, and all the people who love me.

I can think about God's heaven, where people live forever.
I can believe that one day I will be in heaven, too.
I can love God as *God*!

I love God!

Sometimes as a Friend.

Sometimes as a Father.

Sometimes as God.

FILL IN THE MISSING WORDS IN THE PRAYER BELOW. WHEN IT IS FINISHED, YOU CAN CUT IT OUT AND SAVE IT TO SAY EVERY TIME YOU WANT TO TELL GOD ABOUT YOUR LOVE.

DEAR GOD, I LOVE YOU VERY MUCH.

I LOVE YOU AS A ________________ BECAUSE YOU LISTEN TO ME WHEN ___________________________.

I LOVE YOU AS A ______________, TOO, BECAUSE YOU WATCH OVER ME EVERY DAY AND TAKE CARE OF ME WHEN ________________.

I LOVE YOU AS MY ______________, MAKER OF ALL THINGS.

I SEE THE WONDER OF YOUR LOVE WHENEVER I LOOK AT ______________________________.

I LOVE YOU WITH MY WHOLE HEART, WITH MY WHOLE MIND, AND WITH MY WHOLE SOUL.

THANK YOU FOR BEING MY GOD.

AMEN

To the Teacher

Sometimes, loving God means making difficult choices. Here is a play your class can act out about a special choice made by four of Jesus' apostles.

To the Parents

Children are great "givers." When a child has picked a flower for Mom, his or her delight almost bursts forth. A picture drawn for Grandma or a surprise hug for Dad are given from the heart.

This week, the children are learning ways that they can "give" back to God some of the love given to them. To utilize this giving streak in their nature, plan a special celebration of their love for God. It can be a meal or a party. Balloons and streamers can help give a party air to your celebration, but simple decorations made by the children are just as effective and far more personal.

Have your children plan a "surprise" for God, a gift made by their own hands. You can help by giving a few ideas (write a prayer, draw a picture, make a small banner), but the final decision should be made by the children.

Jesus by the Sea

Based on Luke 5:1-11

Cast: Narrator, Simon Peter, Andrew, James, John, Jesus, First Woman, Second Woman, the crowd, a few fishermen along the shore.

Setting: The shores of Galilee.

Props: Two large nets (an old sheet cut in two will work well, or the children can pantomime holding the nets), a background mural of the sea, two large cardboard cartons painted to represent boats.

Narrator: The play opens with Simon Peter and Andrew washing nets in the water. Not too far away are James and John. Jesus is a short way off, talking to a crowd of people.

Simon Peter: Well, Andrew, it wasn't a good night. I'm tired and we've caught nothing. Let's wash these nets and go home.

Andrew: Right you are, brother.

(James and John nod in agreement.)

Narrator: Jesus walks up to the shoreline and climbs into Simon Peter's boat. The crowd becomes concerned that Jesus is going away.

First Woman: Is he leaving? I want to hear more about God. This man makes sense when he talks.

Second Woman: No, I don't think he's leaving. He just wants to push off from shore a little so we can see him better.

Narrator: Jesus sat in the boat and talked to the crowd of people. He told them about his Father and explained things to them that they had never understood before. Then he spoke to Simon Peter.

Jesus: Put out into the deep water and lower your nets for a catch.

Simon Peter: Master, we have been hard at it all night long and have caught nothing. But if you say so, I will lower the nets.

Narrator: Simon Peter and Andrew drop their nets over the side of the boat.

Simon Peter *(in surprise)***:** Andrew, will you look at those nets? They are so full of fish they are going to break!

Andrew: I see them, brother. I can't believe it!

Narrator: Simon Peter and Andrew pull in their nets with great effort. Then Andrew yells to James and John.

Andrew: James! John! Help us! We have too many fish to put into our small boat.

James: John, will you look at all those fish!

Narrator: James throws his net into the sea next to Simon Peter's, then he and John pull it in, struggling to lift it because it is so full.

John: Our boats are both full. Where did those fish come from? It's a miracle!

Simon Peter *(falling to his knees)***:** Leave me, Lord. I am too sinful to be here with you.

Jesus *(lifting Simon Peter to his feet and speaking to all present)***:** Do not be afraid, from now on, you will catch people.

Narrator: Jesus begins to walk away slowly. Simon Peter, Andrew, James, and John throw their nets back into their boats and follow him. They chose to follow Jesus for the rest of their lives.

From the Catechism of the Catholic Church

- #2637, #2639-43 on praise and thanksgiving
- #2633 on times of need
- #2052-55 on the Ten Commandments and the Great Commandment
- #1524-25 on Eucharist and eternal life

Editor: Lauren K. Borstell. Art and design: Christine Kraus.

B E E C C I A O U U S S E I Y N O M U Y A E R Y E E P S R

Circle of God's Love

Use the space outside of the circle to draw some of the things that remind you of God's love for you. Then, if you read every other letter around the circle, starting at the arrow, God will tell you why you are so loved.

_ _ _ _ _ _ _

_ _ _   _ _ _

_ _ _ _ _ _ _ _

_ _   _ _

_ _ _ _.

To the Teacher

Make a Scrapbook of God's Love

For this project, each child will need:

- Hole punch
- Scissors
- Glue
- Old magazines
- Four or five pieces of 8 1/2" x 11" drawing paper or construction paper
- Crayons or markers
- 12" – 15" pieces of yarn

Direct the children through the following steps:

1. Hold all four or five pieces of paper together and fold them in half to make a book.

2. Punch holes on the folded edge and string the yarn through the holes to hold the book together.

3. On the cover of the book, write, "My Book of God's Gifts."

4. Look through magazines to find pictures that are reminders of God's love.

5. Glue a different gift on each page of the book. Beneath the pictures, write a thank-you prayer for that special gift.

Editor: Lauren K. Borstell
Art and design: Christine Kraus
Published with ecclesiastical approval.

Phone: 800-325-9521. Web: Liguori.org.

To the Parents

As the children begin their journey toward an understanding of God's forgiveness, they must first be made fully aware of God's love for them and of the many ways that this love is shown in their daily lives. You, as parents, have countless opportunities to point out the signs of God's love for them.

An excellent family project for this week is a "faith walk" in a wooded area or park. In preparation for this project, decorate a shoe box with pictures cut from a magazine. You can print "God Made the World for Me" on your box.

On the day of your walk, have the children carry bags to collect small mementos: acorns, leaves, birds' feathers, small stones, flower petals, and so forth. During your walk, point out signs of God's love that the children may miss, but give them the opportunity to discover some of these signs on their own.

After your walk, read about the wild flowers in the Sermon on the Mount (see Lk 12:27-28), or the story of creation as found in the Book of Genesis. The children can then store their collections in the decorated box.

From the Catechism of the Catholic Church

- #295,#341 on creation
- #218-21,#733 on God is Love
- #370,#374 on God's attributes and friendship

ISBN 978-0-7648-0194-5

Liguori Publications
A Redemptorist Ministry